The Quotation Bank

Macbeth

William Shakespeare

Copyright © 2022 Esse Publishing Limited

First published in 2016 by:
The Quotation Bank
Esse Publishing Limited

10 9 8 7

A CIP catalogue record for this book is available from the British Library.
ISBN 978-0-9956086-0-3

All enquiries to: contact@thequotationbank.co.uk

Printed and bound by Target Print Limited, Broad Lane, Cottenham, Cambridge CB24 8SW.

www.thequotationbank.co.uk

Introduction

Quotations

Revision and Essay Planning

Welcome to The Quotation Bank, the comprehensive guide to all the key quotations you need to succeed in your exams.

Whilst you may have read the play, watched a production, understood the plot and have a strong grasp of context, the vast majority of marks awarded in your GCSE are for the ability to write a focused essay, full of quotations, and most importantly, quotations that you then analyse.

I think we all agree it is **analysis** that is the tricky part – and that is why we are here to help!

The Quotation Bank takes 25 of the most important quotations from the text, interprets them, analyses them, highlights literary techniques Shakespeare has used, puts them in context, and suggests which quotations you might use in which essays.

At the end of **The Quotation Bank** we have put together a sample answer, essay plans and great revision exercises to help you prepare for your exam. We have also included a detailed glossary to make sure you completely understand what certain literary terms actually mean!

English Literature 9-1: What are examiners looking for?

All GCSE Exam Boards mark your exams using the same Assessment Objectives (AOs) – around 80% of your mark across the English Literature GCSE will be awarded for A01 and A02.

A01	Read, understand and respond to texts. Students should be able to: <ul><li>Maintain a critical style and develop an *informed personal response*</li><li>Use textual references, *including quotations*, to support and illustrate *interpretations*.</li></ul>
A02	Analyse the *Language, Form and Structure* used by a writer to *create meanings and effects*, using *relevant subject terminology* where appropriate.

Basically, **AO1** is the ability to answer the question set, showing a good knowledge of the text, and using quotations to back up ideas and interpretations.

AO2 is the ability to analyse these quotations, as well as the literary techniques the writer uses, and to show you understand the effect of these on the audience.

We will also highlight elements of **AO3** – the context in which the play is set.

How The Quotation Bank can help you in your exams.

The Quotation Bank is designed to make sure that every point you make in an essay clearly fulfils the Assessment Objectives an examiner will be using when marking your work.

Every quotation comes with the following detailed material:

Interpretation: The interpretation of each quotation allows you to fulfil **AO1**, responding to the text and giving an informed personal response.

Techniques: Using subject-specific terminology correctly (in this case, the literary devices used by Shakespeare) is a key part of **AO2**.

Analysis: We have provided as much analysis (**AO2**) as possible. It is a great idea to analyse the quotation in detail – you need to do more than just say what it means, but also what effect the language, form and structure has on the audience.

Use in essays on… Your answer needs to be focused to fulfil **AO1**. This section helps you choose relevant quotations and link them together for a stronger essay.

How to use The Quotation Bank.

Many students spend time learning quotations by heart.

This is an excellent idea, but they often forget what they are meant to do with those quotations once they get into the exam!

By using **The Quotation Bank**, not only will you have a huge number of quotations to use in your essays, you will also have ideas on what to say about them, how to analyse them, how to link them together, and what questions to use them for.

For GCSE essay questions, these quotations can form the basis of your answer, making sure every point comes **directly from the text (AO1)** and allowing you to **analyse language, form and structure (AO2)**. We also highlight where you can easily and effectively include **context (AO3)**.

For GCSE questions that give you an extract to analyse, the quotations in **The Quotation Bank** are excellent not only for revising the skills of **analysis (AO2)**, but also for showing **wider understanding of the text (AO1)**.

ne Scene One:

WITCHES: "Fair is foul, and foul is fair."

Interpretation: From the beginning of the play the audience see that what is right can be wrong, and what is wrong can be right. Boundaries between good and evil are blurred and confused.

Techniques: Alliteration, Repetition.

Analysis:
- The alliteration of the "f" sound creates a sinister, uneasy tone.
- The repetition of "fair" and "foul" suggests the two ideas are interchangeable, emphasised further by the definite "is".
- "Foul" is more dominant and intimidating than "fair" is caring and pleasant – the evil element overpowers goodness.
- The King at the time, James I, wrote a book stating all magic was evil – this chant sounds almost like a magical spell, and the audience would fear it.

Use in essays on… Good versus evil; Morality; The Supernatural; The Witches.

Act One Scene Two:
> SERGEANT: "As cannons over-charged with double cracks."

Interpretation: The Sergeant gives his report on the battle that has just occurred, and Banquo and Macbeth's role in it. The audience's first impression of Macbeth is as a great warrior, a heroic character who is fierce and valiant on the battlefield.

Techniques: Simile; Alliteration.

Analysis:
- Vocabulary such as "cannon" and "charged" gives the audience a sense of Macbeth's explosive, violent power, as if he himself was a powerful weapon who is highly capable of killing.
- The alliteration of the strong "c" sound mimics the dynamic movements of Macbeth through the battlefield.
- The use of "over" and "double" highlights Macbeth has far more value than a typical soldier – he stands above the rest.

Use in essays on…Macbeth; Kingship; Violence; Power.

Scene Five:
LADY MACBETH: "Too full of the milk of human kindness."

Interpretation: Lady Macbeth believes Macbeth does not have the ruthless nature required to become king. Through this statement the audience come to believe she is the driving force behind the events of the play.

Techniques: Imagery; Language.

Analysis:
- The suggestion Macbeth is "too full" implies he is not only good-natured, but he is "too" full – it will stop him achieving the crown.
- The image of "milk" has associations with a comforting and soothing nature – not the qualities Lady Macbeth thinks are required to become king. In Shakespearean context, it should be women who are gentle and kind, not men.
- It is significant she uses the phrase "human" kindness – she implies Macbeth needs to be inhuman, perhaps even supernatural like the witches, if he is to succeed.

Use in essays on…Lady Macbeth; Gender; Ambition; Macbeth; Power.

Act One Scene Five:
  LADY MACBETH: "Come, you spirits/that tend on mortal thoughts, unsex me here!/And fill me, from the crown to the toe, top-full/Of direst cruelty!"

Interpretation: Lady Macbeth believes she must reject her womanly nature if she is to help Macbeth – she also suggests the only way to gain power is through a commitment to evil rather than positive actions.

Techniques: Language.

Analysis:

- The fact that Lady Macbeth invites the spirits with the phrase "Come, you spirits" shows she has embraced the supernatural whereas Macbeth seems nervous of its power.
- The phrase "unsex me here" is an explicit rejection of traditionally female behaviour. Lady Macbeth is rejecting the typical patriarchal society of the time.
- Not only is Lady Macbeth prepared to be cruel, but the adjective "direst" highlights the extreme lengths she is willing to go to.

Use in essays on…Gender; The Supernatural; Power; Corruption.

Act One Scene Five:
 LADY MACBETH: "Look like the innocent flower/But be the serpent under't."

Interpretation: Lady Macbeth shows that manipulation and deceit are the most effective methods of gaining power.

Techniques: Imagery; Juxtaposition; Religious allusions.

Analysis:

- The imagery of the "innocent flower" highlights the goodness, but also the vulnerability, of honest human behaviour.
- The juxtaposition with "the serpent under't" is a clear biblical reference to the serpent in the Garden of Eden, who helped to bring original sin into the world. The audience would certainly link this with the Devil.
- This suggests Lady Macbeth would rather act like the devil than as a moral human being – like the witches, she sees that "fair is foul, and foul is fair."
- The word "under't" implies evil is underneath all of our behaviour.

Use in essays on…Good versus evil; Corruption; Sin; Religion.

Act One Scene Seven:
LADY MACBETH: "I would, while it was smiling in my face,/Have plucked my nipple from his boneless gums,/And dashed the brains out."

Interpretation: Producing and caring for children was a main role for women – Lady Macbeth states she would cruelly reject, even destroy, her child in the pursuit for power.

Techniques: Imagery; Language.

Analysis:
- Lady Macbeth's ability to feel no guilt is highlighted by the fact she believes she could kill her child even if it were "smiling in my face", also showing her willingness to destroy something innocent.
- Her ruthless nature is accentuated by the speed with which she is willing to act – the words "plucked" and "dashed" both suggest swift, clinical movements.
- The use of the phrase "dashed the brains out" foreshadows the horrors acted upon children later in the play. She is again rejecting her traditional womanly role as a mother.

Use in essays on…Gender; Lady Macbeth; Violence; Morality.

Act Two Scene One:
MACBETH: "Is this a dagger which I see before me?"

Interpretation: Macbeth is hallucinating, showing the deterioration of his state of mind and the influences the witches and Lady Macbeth have had on him.

Techniques: Questioning.

Analysis:
- The question "Is this" is representative of Macbeth's state of mind – he is full of uncertainty and doubt.
- The fact that it is a "dagger" before him suggests his mind has become corrupted by violence – the handle of the dagger is pointing towards his hand, almost inviting him to use it.
- In a patriarchal society, male leaders are not meant to have doubt – they are meant to be powerful, certain and strong. Macbeth has become a weaker warrior since the warfare on the battlefields in Act One.

Use in essays on…Violence; The Supernatural; Macbeth; Madness.

13

Act Two Scene Two:
   MACBETH: "But wherefore could not I pronounce Amen?/I had most need of blessing, and Amen/Stuck in my throat."

Interpretation: Doubt, confusion and guilt have now overcome Macbeth. The fact that he cannot say "Amen" shows the audience that Macbeth's actions have separated him from religion, something that could strike fear into a Shakespearean audience with a strong Christian belief.

Techniques: Questioning; Repetition.

Analysis:
- Much like "Is this a dagger which I see before me?" the question is representative of Macbeth's state of mind – he is full of uncertainty and doubt. His hesitancy contrasts greatly with the active behaviour of Lady Macbeth.
- The repetition of "Amen" brings religion to the audience's attention – the fact it "stuck in [his] throat" implies Macbeth has acted so evilly that religion has turned against him – evil cannot co-exist with religion.

Use in essays on…Good versus evil; Religion; The Supernatural; Madness.

Act Two Scene Two:
LADY MACBETH: "A little water clears us of this deed."

Interpretation: Lady Macbeth has to become more ruthless as Macbeth's courage begins to fade – she believes she can simply wash away any sense of guilt for the murders.

Techniques: Language; Pronoun.

Analysis:

- The use of the word "little" highlights just how insignificant murder is to Lady Macbeth, if only a "little water" is needed to wash it away.
- The fact that she believes washing their hands "clears us of the deed" suggests she would only feel regret if they were caught – "clears" implies she has got away with murder.
- She refers to "us" – in a patriarchal society, she sees herself as equal to her husband, and much like the witches, the audience see a powerful woman controlling Macbeth's actions.

Use in essays on…Justice; Sin; Morality.

15

Act Two Scene Four:
  OLD MAN: "A falcon, towering in her pride of place,/Was by a mousing owl hawked at, and killed."

Interpretation: The natural order of things has become subverted – small owls are now killing falcons. It suggests the behaviour of Macbeth has become so unnatural it has caused the natural world to fall apart and the natural order of things to go wrong.

Techniques: Imagery; Symbolism.

Analysis:
- Just like kings should never be killed by their subjects, powerful falcons should not be killed by weak owls.
- Hierarchy was vital to a country's stability. The Divine Right of Kings (the belief Kings were God's voice on earth) meant hierarchy should not be challenged.
- The idea of a "mousing" owl, with associations of small size and lack of strength, killing a "towering" falcon, suggesting power and immense size, links with the unnatural idea of Macbeth killing the King.

Use in essays on… The Supernatural; Power.

Act Three Scene Two:
  LADY MACBETH: "Sleek o'er your rugged looks./Be bright and jovial among your guests tonight."

Interpretation: Macbeth is beginning to lose his mind – Lady Macbeth understands that as long as he looks in control, power will remain in their hands due to the hierarchal system in which they live.

Techniques: Juxtaposition.

Analysis:
- The juxtaposition of "rugged" and "jovial" links to hypocrisy and the two-faced nature of Macbeth's behaviour.
- "Sleek o'er" creates an image of taking something ugly and unpleasant and giving it an appearance of positivity – to be King, Macbeth must look the part.
- The fact that his actions are "rugged", suggesting violence, but his current behaviour is "jovial", with associations of friendship and togetherness, reminds the audience of his deceitful nature.

Use in essays on... Macbeth; Good versus evil; Appearance and reality; Kingship.

Act Three Scene Four:
 MACBETH: "Whole as the marble, founded as the rock…but now I am cabined, cribbed, confined."

Interpretation: This quotation links back to the very beginning of the play. Macbeth was a true warrior, but now he is a weak, vulnerable man.

Techniques: Imagery; Alliteration; Tri-colon (or list of three).

Analysis:

- The first part of the quotation shows Macbeth as he used to be.
- The word "whole" suggests he was the complete soldier, and the associations with "marble" and "rock" are of strong, unbreakable, natural substances – all the things Macbeth used to be, a traditionally strong male.
- The tri-colon of "cabined, cribbed, confined" suggests a feeling of claustrophobia and restriction, as if Macbeth has nowhere to hide and is now vulnerable, emphasised by the alliteration.

Use in essays on…Power; Madness.

Act Three Scene Four:
   MACBETH: "There the grown serpent lies: the worm, that's fled,/Hath nature
that in time will venom breed."

Interpretation: Macbeth realises, in failing to kill Fleance, he has allowed evil and poisonous thoughts to grow against his reign as king. Macbeth also understands that within human nature is the threat of evil corrupting someone's soul.

Techniques: Imagery; Religious allusion.

Analysis:
- Macbeth initially describes Fleance as a "worm", suggesting something that is small and helpless.
- However, he suggests it will grow into a "serpent", linking back to the original sin of Adam and Eve, and will "breed" poison, emphasising to the audience that the anger and violence in the play will grow and develop even further.
- "Will" confirms that these events are inevitable – evil is unstoppable, and "will" lead to poisonous consequences.

Use in essays on…Evil; Corruption; Revenge and justice.

Act Three Scene Four:
   MACBETH: "Prithee, see there! Behold! Look! Lo! How say you?/Why – what care I?"

Interpretation: Macbeth has lost all control over his surroundings. He is now confused and frightened, unsure of what is occurring around him.

Techniques: Sentence structure; Prose.

Analysis:
- Most of Shakespeare's characters, and definitely his powerful characters, speak in Iambic Pentameter, and certainly in verse. However, Macbeth's sentences have become stuttering, fractured and broken. He is now speaking in basic, usually monosyllabic words, and in prose, language only usually spoken by Shakespeare's uneducated characters (see the Porter for an example in Act Two Scene Three).
- His mind has become destroyed, and his language is now unintelligent and unfocused.

Use in essays on…The Supernatural; Power; Madness.

cene Five:
CATE: "This night I'll spend/Unto a dismal and a fatal end."

ion: The most powerful witch of all, Hecate, is intent on making sure that
the outcome of the action is both painful and deadly. It will be a truly tragic end. The
audience may well have a strong belief in fate – they would fear that their own life is not
necessarily in their control.

Techniques: Language; Sentence structure.

Analysis:

- The idea of Hecate saying she will "spend" a night on Macbeth's fate suggests she is in full control of what happens to him – it has associations with careful planning and scheming to ensure his "fatal end".
- The use of "dismal" and "fatal" show that Macbeth's fate is going to result in death, but "dismal" also implies an unheroic end for a once great soldier.
- The fact Hecate states that she wants "a dismal <u>and</u> a fatal end", rather than 'dismal, fatal end' lengthens the sentence and extends the pain Macbeth will feel.

Use in essays on… Power; The Supernatural; The Witches; Fate.

Act Four Scene One:
    WITCH: "Finger of birth-strangled babe,/Ditch-delivered by a drab."

Interpretation: This is just one of the many horrific ingredients that go into the witches' cauldron. The idea of including body parts from a dead baby shows just how evil the witches truly are, and that Macbeth was always going to be defeated by their horrific magic.

Techniques: Language; Imagery; Alliteration.

Analysis:
- This list of ingredients around the dark cauldron is at its most evil when the finger of a "babe" is added, a symbol of pure innocence being destroyed, linking to the destruction of the previously good Macbeth.
- The image of it being "birth-strangled" highlights the extreme cruelty of the witches.
- The alliteration of the "b" and "d" sounds creates a chant-like tone to the list of ingredients, accentuating the supernatural feel.

Use in essays on…The Supernatural; The Witches; Good versus evil.

Act Four Scene One:
> **MACBETH: "Though you untie the winds and let them fight/Against the churches."**

Interpretation: The completely unnatural behaviour of the witches is so powerful that it has even turned the natural world against religion, causing conflict throughout the land.

Techniques: Personification; Pathetic fallacy.

Analysis:
- Here the churches are a personified symbol of morality and goodness – it would be distressing for the religious audience to see Christianity attacked in this way.
- The witches have deliberately turned the wind against it, with the word "fight" linking to the violent conflicts throughout the play.
- The fact they "untie" the winds has associations with a great power being unleashed against the moral goodness of the Church. Because the wind is attacking "against the churches" it seems as if the Church is passive and vulnerable to evil's power.

Use in essays on…Religion; The Witches; Good versus evil; Violence.

Act Four Scene One:
  MACBETH: "Then live, Macduff. What need I fear of thee?/But yet I'll make
      assurance double sure,/And take a bond of fate: thou shalt not live."

Interpretation: Macbeth is trying to maintain control over his own life. He believes that by killing Macduff, he is guiding his own fate.

Techniques: Sentence structure; Language.

Analysis:
- Macbeth's nervousness and fragility is evident here – rather than the brave warrior from the beginning of the play, now he is desperate to be "sure" and needs "assurance".
- It also shows the conflict in his mind – he starts by suggesting that Macduff can "live", but follows this with a question, and then a complete contradiction, saying "thou shalt not live".
- We also see Macbeth's lack of actual power as he needs to "take a bond of fate", relying on fate to assist him.

Use in essays on…Violence; Fate; Power; Corruption.

Act Four Scene Three:
ROSS: "Your wife and babes/Savagely slaughtered."

Interpretation: The image of violence flows through this statement, with the lengths Macbeth is now willing to go to in his quest for power evident to the audience. There is a clear difference between the murders earlier in the play and the deaths of Macduff's family.

Techniques: Sibilance; Juxtaposition.

Analysis:
- The juxtaposition of "wife and babes", images of innocence, love and care, being "savagely slaughtered" (the word savage suggesting an almost inhuman behaviour) indicates to the audience the level of violence and evil Macbeth now engages in.
- The sibilance of "savagely slaughtered" adds a swiftness to the sentence, a clear development from the hesitancy he showed before he killed Duncan.

Use in essays on…Violence; Power; Good versus evil; Revenge and justice.

Act Four Scene Three:
   Malcolm: "let grief/Convert to anger. Blunt not the heart, enrage it."

Interpretation: The audience can see here that the culmination of the play will be violent and bloody – Malcolm insists that Macduff not feel sorrow, but instead use his pain to exact revenge.

Techniques: Language; Personification.

Analysis:
- The use of emotive language shows the audience how emotionally charged the final acts will be – the abstract nouns "grief" and "anger" are a dangerous mix of sorrow and fury.
- Malcolm compels Macduff to make sure his heart, with its associations of goodness or bravery, becomes enraged, suggesting behaviour that feels no remorse. He needs to act in a stereotypically masculine way.
- Malcolm personifies Macduff's heart, demanding he "enrage it", as if it were another soldier in the battle against Macbeth.

Use in essays on… Violence; Revenge and justice; Good versus evil.

Act Five Scene One:
LADY MACBETH: "Out, damned spot!"

Interpretation: Lady Macbeth has lost all of her composure and rational thought from earlier in the play – like Macbeth in Act Two, her mind has begun to hallucinate.

Techniques: Sentence structure; Religious allusion; Irony.

Analysis:
- In Act Two, Lady Macbeth claims that, after killing King Duncan, "a little water clears us of this deed."
- Now she is hallucinating, and desperately pleads for the blood to be washed away. It is ironic that when Macbeth desperately needed to clean his hands Lady Macbeth mocked him, but guilt is now having the same effect upon her behaviour.
- The fact she describes the blood spot as "damned" has associations with hell – her guilt has caught her, and she fears she is being punished. The religious audience could see this as divine punishment from God.

Use in essays on…The Supernatural; Religion; Fate.

Act Five Scene Three:
   MACBETH: "The mind I sway by, and the heart I bear,/Shall never sag wit.
                  doubt, nor shake with fear."

Interpretation: Macbeth has come full circle, and has returned to his former warrior self – he is displaying typical characteristics of a powerful leader once more. Although he is now full of evil intentions, his spirit is as strong as ever.

Techniques: Language.

Analysis:
- In previous acts, Macbeth was riddled with "doubt" and "fear" – now the word "never" is positioned before it, showing he has finally regained control over his own behaviour.
- He is again in full control, as shown by the reference to both "mind", suggesting his thoughts, and "heart", emphasising his emotions.
- "Sag" and "shake" both suggest weak body movements, something Macbeth explicitly rejects.

Use in essays on…Power; Kingship.

Five

MACBETH: "Life's but a walking shadow."

n: Macbeth has had an epiphany (a moment of realisation) and suggests
   o real substance to it – it is simply a "shadow."

Techniques: Metaphor; Sentence structure.

Analysis:
- The use of the metaphor depicting life as a "shadow" suggests life is empty and has no meaning – it also has associations with following (our shadow follows us around) as if we are simply following someone else's plan.
- The use of "walking" implies life is a journey, but not a dynamic, energetic one – walking is not the powerful, physical action seen in earlier acts, nor the dynamic action expected of a King.
- The sentence structure focuses on the word "but", meaning only or just. Macbeth is arguing that life is worthless – it is only a shadow.

Use in essays on…Power; Fate; Morality; Identity.

Act Five Scene Five:
    MACBETH: "A poor player/That struts and frets his hour upon the stage."

Interpretation: Macbeth understands he is under the control of someone, or something, else. He is simply an actor ("player") who has his life controlled by the witches, and then he will be forgotten.

Techniques: Metaphor; Alliteration.

Analysis:
- The image of Macbeth as a "poor player" contrasts the previous image of him as a powerful "cannon" in Act One. Here the alliteration adds to the pitiful nature of his character.
- The verbs "struts" and "frets" are both weak, indecisive actions – they suggest lack of control and power.
- The fact that we only have an "hour upon the stage" emphasises how fleeting and insignificant each person is, foreshadowing the death that is to come.

Use in essays on…Power; Fate; Identity.

Act Five Scene Eight:
> MACDUFF: "I have no words;/My voice is in my sword."

Interpretation: Macduff realises that justice can only be achieved through fighting, not through words – he must meet Macbeth's violent deeds with violence of his own to avenge the death of his family.

Techniques: Personification.

Analysis:

- Macduff cannot put into words the pain he feels at Macbeth's actions, and he acts in the way Lady Macbeth suggested men should earlier in the play – with actions, not words.
- His "sword" has become his "voice" – in killing Macbeth, he says everything he needs to so as to deliver justice and revenge.
- The idea of his voice being "in" his sword suggests the sword is more than just a physical weapon – it contains all of the anger and hatred of Macbeth's victims, adding to its strength.

Use in essays on…Violence; Revenge and justice; Power.

Major Themes

The Supernatural	Appearance and Reality	Gender and Identity
Sin and Morality	Revenge and Justice	Fate
Ambition	Good versus Evil	Violence
Kingship	Corruption	Loyalty
Religion	Madness	Power

Major Characters

Macbeth	Lady Macbeth	King Duncan
Macduff	Lady Macduff	The Witches
Banquo	Fleance	Malcolm

How to revise effectively.

One mistake people often make is to try to revise EVERYTHING!

This is clearly not possible.

Instead, once you know and understand the plot, a great idea is to pick three or four major themes, and three or four major characters, and revise these in great detail.

If, for example, you revised Lady Macbeth and The Witches, you will also have covered a huge amount of material to use in questions about Gender, Sin or Evil.

Or, if you revised Good versus Evil and Power, you would certainly have plenty of material if a question on Macbeth, Banquo or Conflict was set.

Use the following framework as a basis for setting **any** of your own revision questions – simply swap the theme or character to create a new essay title!

How does Shakespeare portray the theme of _____ in *Macbeth*?

How does the character of _____ develop as the play progresses?

A sample essay paragraph (top level), using ideas directly from
The Quotation Bank (page 9).

How far do you agree that Shakespeare presents Lady Macbeth as ambitious?

Lady Macbeth is clearly an ambitious woman, and Shakespeare presents her as determined to succeed, particularly through her language choice and imagery. When she claims that Macbeth is <u>"too full of the milk of human kindness"</u>, the suggestion is that Macbeth does not have the drive to succeed; the image of <u>"milk"</u> has comforting, soothing qualities, perhaps linking with femininity, and the phrase <u>"human kindness"</u> implies she is willing to be inhuman to achieve her ambitions, much like the witches. She takes the ambitious plans even further when she cries <u>"Come, you spirits/...unsex me here!"</u> Lady Macbeth believes she must reject her womanly nature if she is to help Macbeth; she also suggests the only way to gain power is through a commitment to evil rather than positive means. The fact that Lady Macbeth invites the spirits with the phrase <u>"Come, you spirits"</u> shows she has embraced the supernatural, whereas Macbeth seems nervous of its power. The phrase <u>"unsex me here"</u> is an explicit rejection of traditionally female behaviour. Not only is Lady Macbeth prepared to be cruel to achieve her ambitions, but the adjective <u>"direst"</u> highlights the extreme lengths she is willing to go to.

Potential Essay Questions

How does Shakespeare explore the concept of sin in *Macbeth*?

Topic Sentence 1: Sin is explicitly linked with religion.

Use: Pages 14 and 23.

Topic Sentence 2: Shakespeare depicts some extreme examples of sinful acts, for example violence against innocent children.

Use: Pages 12, 19 and 22.

Topic Sentence 3: Furthermore, sin frequently develops when a character is exposed to the supernatural elements of the play.

Use: Pages 7 and 10.

Topic Sentence 4: The consequence of sin seems to be a descent into madness.

Use: Pages 20 and 27.

How is the idea of power portrayed in *Macbeth*?

Topic Sentence 1: Power is often shown in Macbeth as meaning physical power and strength, frequently seen in scenes of violence and fighting.

Use: Pages 8, 10 and 31.

Topic Sentence 2: In contrast to physical power, Shakespeare also portrays the ability to manipulate others as the way to obtain power.

Use: Pages 11 and 21.

Topic Sentence 3: Once power is gained, it is frequently portrayed as something that characters desperately try to hold on to.

Use: Pages 17 and 24.

Topic Sentence 4: However, at the conclusion of the play, Shakespeare portrays power as essentially non-existent.

Use: Pages 29 and 30.

How is the supernatural depicted in *Macbeth*?

Topic Sentence 1: The most obvious way the supernatural is depicted is as inhuman and unnatural.

Use: Pages 10, 16 and 22.

Topic Sentence 2: What makes the supernatural more disturbing is the powerful and controlling nature of it – it physically makes people see things that aren't there.

Use: Pages 13 and 27.

Topic Sentence 3: For Shakespeare's audience, it is particularly troubling when the supernatural is depicted as battling against religion.

Use: Pages 14 and 23.

Topic Sentence 4: Whether or not the supernatural can overpower people, it is clearly depicted as being able to control the fate of the characters in the play.

Use: Pages 21, 29 and 30.

How does Macbeth develop throughout the play?

Topic Sentence 1: Macbeth is introduced to the audience as a strong and powerful warrior.

Use: Pages 8 and 28.

Topic Sentence 2: Despite his military honour, Macbeth becomes manipulative, deceitful and corrupt in his quest for power.

Use: Pages 17 and 24.

Topic Sentence 3: As well as being a powerful soldier and an ambitious king, he could also be seen as weak and vulnerable.

Use: Pages 9, 18 and 20.

Topic Sentence 4: Essentially, Macbeth develops into a victim of fate.

Use: Pages 14, 21 and 29.

Suggested Revision Activities

Major character and themes – Take any of the major characters and themes (see page 32 for a list) and group together quotations in sets of 2 or 3 to answer the following question: "How does the theme/character develop as the play goes on?"

You should try to get 4 sets of quotations, giving you 8-12 overall.

A great cover and repeat exercise – Cover the whole page, apart from the quotation at the top. Can you now fill in the four sections in your exercise book without looking – Interpretations, Techniques, Analysis, Use in essays on...?

This also works really well as a revision activity with a friend – cover the whole card, apart from the quotation at the top. If you read out the quotation, can they tell you the four sections without looking – Interpretations, Techniques, Analysis, Use in essays on...?

"The Development Game" – Pick any quotation at random from The Quotation Bank and use it to create an essay question, and then create a focused topic sentence to start the essay. Next, find another appropriate quotation to develop your idea even further.

"The Contrast Game" – Follow the same rules as The Development Game, but instead of finding a quotation to support your idea, find a quotation that can be used to start a counter-argument.

Your very own Quotation Bank! Using the same headings and format as The Quotation Bank, find 10 more quotations from throughout the text (select them from many different sections of the text to help develop whole text knowledge) and create your own revision cards.

Essay writing – They aren't always fun, but writing essays is great revision. Choose a practice question and then try taking three quotations and writing out a perfect paragraph, making sure you add connectives, technical vocabulary and sophisticated language.

Glossary

Alliteration – Repetition of the same consonant or sound at the beginning of a number of words in a sentence: "fair is foul, and foul is fair" creates a threatening chanting sound.

Allusions – Referring to something in a sentence without mentioning it explicitly: "be the serpent under't" alludes to the snake in the Garden of Eden, therefore links Macbeth with sin.

Imagery – Figurative language that appeals to the senses of the audience: "whole as the marble" creates a hard, cold feeling, just like Macbeth's character.

Juxtaposition – Two ideas, images or words placed next to each other to create a contrasting effect: "Flower" and "Serpent" are used together to highlight beauty and evil together.

Language – The vocabulary chosen to create effect.

Metaphor – A word or phrase used to describe something else so that the first idea takes on the associations of the second: "life's but a walking shadow" means life takes on the empty, dark associations of a shadow.

Pathetic Fallacy – The weather or environment mimics the mood or actions of the play to enhance the effect: "untie the winds and let them fight" shows the physical environment increasing the atmosphere of conflict in the play.

Personification – A non-human object or concept takes on human qualities to make its presence more vivid to the audience: "though you untie the winds and let them fight/Against the churches" creates an image of the wind physically attacking the church.

Prose – Normal spoken or written language, instead of verse. Usually, only Shakespeare's uneducated characters (like the Porter) speak in prose – when powerful characters do it shows them losing control.

Repetition – When a word, phrase or idea is repeated to reinforce it: "fair" and "foul" are repeated to reinforce the conflict between them throughout the play.

Rhetorical Questions – A persuasive device where the person asking the question already knows the answer: "Are you a man?" forces Macbeth to act in a stereotypically masculine way to prove himself.

Sentence Structure – The way the writer has ordered the words in a sentence to create a certain effect: "thou shalt not live" stresses the word "not", emphasising Macbeth's intention to kill Macduff.

Sibilance – A variation on alliteration, usually of the 's' sound, that creates a hissing sound: "savagely slaughtered" creates an evil tone to accompany the evil actions.

Simile – A comparison of one thing with something of a different kind, used to make a description more vivid: Macbeth and Banquo were "as cannons", which makes them take on all of the associations of the weapon.

Symbolism – The use of a symbol to represent an idea: the falcon killed by an owl is a symbol of traditional order being switched around.

Tri-colon – A list of three words or phrases for effect: "cabined, cribbed, confined" powerfully implies the feeling of being trapped that has taken over Macbeth.